101 Top Tips & Techniques for Amazing Presentations

Steve Torjussen
foreword by Dr Peter Honey

101 Top Tips & Techniques for Amazing Presentations
Steve Torjussen

Copyright © 2014 by Steve Torjussen
All Rights Reserved
Cover © 2014 by Alison Jones
Cover image: Microphone by Daehyun Park, used under CC0 licence

All rights reserved. No part of this book may be reproduced in any form by any means without the expressed permission of the authors. This includes reprints, excerpts, photocopying, recording, or any future means of reproducing text. If you would like to do any of the above, please seek permission first by contacting the author.

Published in the United Kingdom by Practical Inspiration Publishing
ISBN 978-1-910056-05-9 (print)
ISBN 978-1-910056-04-2 (ebook)

Table of Contents

About the Author   v
Foreword   vii
Acknowledgements   ix
101 Top Tips & Techniques for Amazing Presentations   1

About the Author

As an experienced presenter, trainer, facilitator and coach Steve knows a thing or two about making presentations. He's been well trained, learnt from making loads of mistakes and sees so many conference speakers and presentations go badly wrong that he's worked out what works and he knows what he's talking about.

He brings over 30 years' experience in public speaking; making sales presentations and pitches; talking in public; training as well as conference speaking in a very wide range of public and private sector organisations. He has unique business experience gained within the finance, banking and motor industries and an invaluable understanding of personal and business dynamics, with a genuine talent for business writing that is pragmatic, memorable, effective, inspiring and most of all fun. His Presentation Skills workshops have won high praise and are very much in demand.

Some comments from just one recent course, with only six attendees:

> "Steve was very knowledgable and approachable."

> "The course was great as I could see myself improving over the day – very encouraging!"

> "The information was presented excellently."

> "Well worth the day."

> "Some useful techniques to use in the workplace."

"Excellent overall."

"Very engaging trainer."

"Really enjoyable!! :)"

"Positive for me to have such good feedback."

"Very good trainer giving critique, focusing on positives yet encouraging improvements required."

"Very good day."

To find out more visit [Sales Training Stuff Ltd](), or to contact Steve directly call him on 01789 400745 or email [Steve.torjussen@btinternet.com]().

Foreword

By Dr Peter Honey

Giving a presentation, rather like being interviewed, is special. This is because presentations and interviews are both occasions when your appearance and your behaviour are under close scrutiny. As far as your audience is concerned, you are your behaviour! Like the tip of an iceberg, this is the part of you that shows and, unfair though it is, their impressions of you are largely based on how you behave. I say this is unfair because, of course, you know perfectly well that you are much more than your outward behaviour. As far as you are concerned, you are knowledgeable, you have passionate beliefs, you have integrity.... and so on. But, unfortunately, your audience can't observe these fine qualities; they only have your behaviour to go on.

This is why so much of the advice in this book focuses, not on what you know, but on what you do.

The good news is that the behaviours you need to use to give effective presentations are learnable. If they weren't, there would be no point in reading this book.

Surveys show that the majority of people are fearful of speaking in public. No one was born with this fear (you couldn't have been; you hadn't even heard of presentations when you were born!). If you have a debilitating phobia about public speaking, you can overcome it – as many people already have. The maxim is: 'If you do the thing you fear, the fear will disappear'. Take a deep breath and have a go.... then another go..... then another. Heeding the advice in this book will help you gradually to overcome your fear. I am also a great believer in the 'power of three' (see #20). Don't be daunted by 101 suggestions. Be selective, pick and choose, concentrate on no more than three at a time – even one or two will do.

Skills are mastered gradually by practice. There are no secrets, no magic wands, just hard graft. Self-confidence slowly builds as a consequence of scoring some small successes. Please don't fall into the trap of assuming that you must feel confident before you have a go.

Techniques and effective behaviours come first with confidence running along behind, keen to catch up.

The overall message of this encouraging book is that you can do it!

Acknowledgements

There are so many people to thank here that I fear I may turn this page into a long and unwelcome equivalent of an Oscar speech! To avoid that I will keep it brief and in that way probably more meaningful.

The first person to thank would be my daughter Hannah Hargrave. With a background in publishing and a few years' experience with the BBC she has inspired me to put pen to paper and achieve something I've dreamed about for some time. That's not to say my son Matthew and youngest daughter Sophie haven't inspired me. For this project though Hannah deserves particular credit and recognition.

When I started to write this, little did I think that someone who I hold in the very highest esteem would take note. I met Peter Honey when I invited him to speak to the organisation I was working with some 30 years ago. We've met subsequently and he has always remembered me. He is a great gentleman, a guru in learning and development and I am very grateful to him for his time, encouragement and the foreword that he wrote. I'm truly honoured.

In 2013 I met Alison Jones. She immediately struck me as being a very powerful and effective coach and I was lucky enough to persuade her to help me in this project. Her challenging questions, great support and encouragement have not only helped me complete the book but she has also added huge value to its appearance, style and content. It was a pleasure to work with her and I hope she will agree to help me in many future projects.

During 2013 I started writing a gratitude diary. It was an experiment really, a challenge to myself to find out how I could recognise the wonderful people and things that happen to me. Within a very short time it has taught me that I have many blessings, I should treasure the people around me, and there are lots of things I should be grateful for. I know that those I haven't mentioned here will be written about in my diary as well as my heart.

Thank you all.

101 Top Tips & Techniques for Amazing Presentations

1 Practise
Handling groups of people isn't about knowing what to do: it's about being able to do it. Take every opportunity to demonstrate these new skills so that you can utilise them when required.

2 Learn from Others
Find someone who is already good at presenting and has the success you crave and find out what they do that you don't. Analyse what works and what doesn't work, and incorporate those bits that do work into your own presentations. This process is called modelling.

3 Learn from Yourself
If you have an important presentation to do record yourself, play it back and watch how effective you are and identify the improvements you could make.

> "Being good is good business."
>
> **Anita Roddick**

4 Unconscious Competence
The more you practise, the more automatic your actions will be. Actions we do all the time such as breathing, walking or eating we do instinctively. Keep practising your presentation skills until you achieve that instinctive stage.

5 Find Out How Good You Are
Actively seek feedback from your audience and colleagues to find out how good you are and what you need to improve and change. You may decide not to act on the feedback, but at least you'll know what others think.

6 Always Present Yourself Effectively
Presentation skills aren't just relevant to how you stand up in front of an audience. The skills are also relevant whenever you meet someone. Whether it's a stranger or a friend we are making some kind of impact on them. What's the impact you make?

7 First Impressions are Important
The first 30 seconds of your presentation are crucial. Some will say you've even got less time than that! Most audiences will sum up and make a decision on whether they like you and what you've got to say during the first 30 seconds. Make sure this period is as powerful as you can make it!

8 Dress to Impress
Since you are your most powerful visual aid, what you wear to give your presentation has to be thought through carefully. Is there a dress code? What would your audience expect you to be wearing? Make sure you wear something that fits you well and that you feel comfortable wearing.

9 Grab Your Audience's Attention
You do need to break the ice with your audience immediately. Some suggestions to do this would include the use of humour (but with care, see #92); asking a question to focus their minds; or the use of dramatic statistics or metaphors, and there are many others.

10 Consider the Overall Message
When presenting, you are there to convey a message to your audience. Always think about what you need the audience to agree to, to do differently or to understand. It's the audi-

ence's perception of the message they receive that is most important.

1. Be Explicit About Your Objective

Audiences appreciate openness and honesty. So if you do have an objective of making a sale, tell them. It then goes without saying that when you get to the end you can legitimately ask them if they want to buy from you.

> "Obstacles are things a person sees when he takes his eyes off the goal."
>
> E. Joseph Cossmann

2. How We Communicate

The message we send to others is conveyed in 3 ways:

- The words we use to talk
- The way we deliver those words, eg our voice
- Our physiology or body language

These three together give your audience the overall message that they will be leaving the meeting with. Make sure all three elements are congruent and aligned to improve the clarity of your message.

3. Words Are Only 7%

Yes that's right! Mehrabian's famous research showed that the words of your message actually only equates to 7% of its meaning, and although there is some dispute about the exact figure it's certainly a crucial point . Think about William Shakespeare. If you take one of his best plays Romeo and Juliet and compare the school play production with the Royal Shakespeare production what do you get? Ignoring the price difference, the school play is terrible - even if your kids are in it. The words remain the same but the Royal Shakespeare Company have great skill in bringing the words to life with both the way they say the words, and how they use their physiology to 'live' the part.

14 The Tone of the Voice Is 38%

Again, according to Mehrabian. There is a saying 'It's not what you say that counts, it's how you say it', and how right that is. Think about how you say the words, ensuring the pace is right, the volume is conducive to your message and there is musical variety in your voice. A good speaking voice can really enhance your professional image and stature, as well as hold the attention of your audience.

15 55% of the Impact Is Your Physiology

Your body language has the single biggest influence over the receiver of your message - your audience. Make sure that what your body language is portraying complements and supports your words and voice, and hence the whole message.

16 The Whole Message is Key

Ensure your audience goes away with the idea that your message was really interesting, that you knew what you were talking about, and that they'll take the action you need and want them to take. It's not until all three elements work together that we create the powerful and congruent message that will have the effect on the audience that we want.

> "It's not what you say that counts, it's how you say it."
>
> **Anon**

17 Words Have Power

While I have said that the words affect only 7% of the influence and impact on the audience, they still can be powerful. Words have the power to make grown men cry; they have the power to make them laugh; they even have the power to make wars! Think about them carefully!

18 Use Stories and Your Own Experiences
If you can weave any of your own personal experiences into what you say it can be a very powerful way of communicating. It also allows the audience to relate more closely to you as a person.

19 Avoid Corporate Jargon
Be mindful that your audience may not all know the acronyms, slang and 'shorthand' of your industry or subject. You wouldn't use this language at home so avoid it during your presentation.

20 Power of Three
When you group things together in threes it not only becomes compelling, it's also easily memorable. Consider for instance Abraham Lincoln's speech: 'That a government of the people, by the people, for the people, shall not perish'. Powerful stuff!

21 Repetition of Your Message
Repeating the same word or phrase at the beginning of successive sentences is a powerful way to help your audience remember what you say. A great example of this is Winston Churchill's radio broadcast where he said: 'We shall fight them on the beaches, we shall fight them…   ' – I bet you've already completed the sentence!

22 Contrasting Two Opposing Ideas
Another effective rhetorical technique is to contrast two opposing ideas by placing one next to the other. For example John F Kennedy said: 'Ask not what your country can do for you. Ask what you can do for your country.'

23 Pay Attention to Detail

A good checklist is a useful idea to ensure that all the last-minute preparations are covered, and covered effectively. Overlooking a small detail at the last minute could cost you!

24 The 'Verbals'

These include the volume of your voice; the speed (both when you're speaking and the pauses in between your words); the musical content as well as the articulation of your words. These can greatly increase the interest and appeal of your message.

25 Watch Out for the Fillers

Do you find you use 'fillers' when you speak such as 'um', 'err', 'you know', 'right'? These words are produced almost involuntarily while your brain is synthesising your thoughts. But you can think without saying anything. Indeed sometimes it can be powerful to let your audience know that you are thinking before you say anything. Wouldn't you prefer to have someone say something to you that's been thought through?

26 A Dry Mouth

If your mouth goes dry while speaking, have a glass of water handy to help. This can also be used if someone asks a challenging question. Take a sip, giving yourself time to think, and by the time you've put the glass back down you'll have thought of the best answer.

27 Breathing

The secret to improving your voice quality is through breathing. Even the great opera singers and actors practise breathing techniques to maintain their voice quality. Be conscious of your breathing, take one or two deep, slow breaths to calm yourself before you speak, and stand tall so that your lungs can fill properly as you talk.

"The language of the body is the key that can unlock the soul."

Konstantin Stanislavsky

28 How Do You Stand?

Be aware of how you stand when presenting. Rehearse the way you do it, see yourself in a mirror or video recording and make sure you know how your audience will see you.

29 Move To Add Value to What You Say

While I may give the impression that standing still is best when presenting (at #39 below), some movement can be good to add to your overall message. If you're using a prop as a visual aid then think about and practise how you will walk over to the item and show it to the audience. Don't leave it to chance!

30 Muscles are Highly Effective at Communicating Our Message

Language is a very recent acquisition in our evolution as human beings. Human beings originally only communicated through their body language and their tone by grunting. There are effectively more muscles from the neck up than there are from the neck down. In the face alone there are over 160 muscles that are purely for facial expression. Use them to communicate your message effectively – an animated face is so much more compelling than a deadpan mask.

"In the last analysis, what we are communicates far more eloquently than anything else we say or do."

Stephen R Covey

31 Build Rapport

The quickest and simplest way to build rapport is to make eye contact with your audience. However when we arrive to do a presentation the first thing we notice is everyone is looking at us, and as a result the pattern on the carpet or the colour of the ceiling suddenly takes on a new fascination! In order to give our audience the impression that we are genuinely interested in them and that we are having a series of one-to-one conversations, the following guidelines apply:

- Make eye contact with different individuals with the natural punctuation of the speech
- Randomise the eye contact rather than going from one side of the room to the other and back again
- Don't leave anyone out.

32 Eye Contact

The normal length of eye contact with individuals should be between 3 and 5 seconds. Any longer and it can become a stare and inhibiting. Any shorter and you run the risk of appearing insincere, shifty or downright dishonest!

33 Gauge your audience's reactions

Besides building rapport, when you make good eye contact you can also gauge people's reactions and find out if they are genuinely interested in your message. If not, you've got the choice to do something different to re-engage them.

34 Nervous Energy

Nerves can take over when you're presenting to groups. Often our nerves are conveyed to our audience via body language. What is it that you do that either makes you look nervous or look confident? Whatever the type of meeting that you're running, you will want to appear confident in front of your groups.

35 Fear of Public Speaking
Research indicates that 80% of people fear public speaking. Don't allow this phobia to limit your influence. If you've got a good idea present it with passion, using the tips in this book to overcome your fear.

36 Nerves are Conveyed Through Body Language
Consider what you do with your hands. Do you wave them about aimlessly? Do you fidget with them or fiddle with your fingers? I recommend you keep them relaxed and by your sides until you want to use them to add value to your message.

37 What are Nerves?
Nerves are the messages we hear from our unconscious mind. Believe it or not they are not there to paralyse you and make you fail, although this is often the effect they have. They have a positive intention, and the message that they are trying to convey is: 'Are you prepared for this?'

38 Adrenalin is Good
It is important to recognise that we probably won't want to get rid of the nerves altogether. Some element of nervous energy is important. It's called adrenalin. The moment you arrive to present and you feel no nerves is likely to be the moment you should stop!

39 Confidence, Honesty and Assertion
Three great impacts you will want to demonstrate in front of your audience. The ideal stance for this is to have your feet shoulder/hip width apart, legs straight and no movement from the waist down. The feet should also be pointed slightly outwards.

40 Movement is Good Though
I should emphasise that this does not mean that movement is a bad thing. The key is that all movement is for a purpose, not incidental, and that you should always be aware of the effect that it has on the audience. Movement should not be

about our own comfort as a presenter but more about the effect you wish to have on the audience.

41 Gestures

In a one-to-one conversation we use all sorts of gestures, from hand movement to facial expressions. The thing that needs to change when presenting to a group is the size of the gestures. The larger the group the larger the gesture needs to be.

42 Hands and Arms

Don't forget that when making gestures with your hands you can move your arms not only from your wrists but also from your elbow and shoulder. Which scale of gesture is more likely to support your words and help get your message across to the back of the room?

43 The Descriptive Gesture

Size is easily demonstrated with hand and arm movements. If you're talking about a massive problem to be overcome it's much more effective to stretch the arms out from the shoulder to emphasise the size of the issue rather than placing your hands 5 or 6 inches away from each other.

44 The Rapport Gesture

This gesture is excellent in helping achieve both rapport with individuals and cohesiveness with the entire group. When using a rapport gesture you need to look at the individual whilst delivering the message and extend the arm towards them, keeping the palm of your hand upwards.

> "If you're presenting yourself with confidence, you can pull off pretty much anything."
>
> **Katy Perry**

45 The Nodding Dog
When you would like to achieve agreement you may want to nod as you speak. This can be highly contagious. In the same way as we respond to yawns you'll find it's virtually impossible for individuals not to nod with you!

46 Energy Levels
When your energy is low you'll find that this is reflected in your voice tone, its musical content and volume. Always ensure that you have plenty of energy when presenting and that you show enthusiasm for your subject.

47 Visual Aids
A visual aid is something that is seen by an audience in order to help them reach the presenter's objective. As such the most effective visual aid as a presenter is YOU! Think about where you stand and make sure you're seen by everyone: don't let the PowerPoint slide take over.

48 Helping the Audience
Visuals such as PowerPoint slides are there to help the audience rather than as a crutch for presenters, helping them remember their script. They should add to your message rather than simply provide words you can repeat verbatim.

49 Audience Interaction
Don't be afraid to get your audience involved in some way, for example by a show of hands, inviting questions, a small group exercise, discussion in threes etc. This can be used to build stronger rapport with them as well as encouraging them to have fun. We all like to have fun!

50 Objective
Every presentation should have an objective set out before you start planning what you're going to say. For example:

At the end of my presentation, my audience will...
- understand
- be able to/capability, or
- commit/take action.

What is it that you want the audience to say, do or want?

51 Start With the End in Mind
The quote from Steven Covey above is so relevant. Think about what you want to achieve. Set your objective clearly, then work back from there.

52 Objectives Again
Setting a specific, audience-focused objective is key in preparing and measuring return on investment at the end of the meeting: did you achieve what you needed to achieve?

53 Don't simplify what you say - simplify how you say it
Einstein once said that everything should be made as simple as possible - but no simpler. The more complicated your ideas the more you'll need to find a creative way to explain them. Always think about your audience and how they can take in your ideas. Try analogies, stories, examples or a carefully created graphic.

54 Structure
There are a wide number of structures you could use to prepare your presentation. The simplest is to ensure you've got a great beginning, an interesting middle and a very strong end. Remember in effect you've got to tell your audience what you're going to say, say it, and then tell them what you've said.

55 Know What to Leave Out
One of the most common problems with presentations is that people often don't know what to leave out. This results in them including so much material that they bore the audience to death. If you miss out something important they'll ask you about it, so don't worry!

56 My Presentation

It's personal to you. It should not be a presentation that you've borrowed from someone else or adopted from the 'corporate' slides. Yes, it should reflect the corporate style if there is one, but don't expect your audience to want to sit through dozens of slides that tell them how great your company is. They're more likely to respond with a "So what!".

57 Your Audience

When considering how realistic the objective is, what sort of things do you need to know about your audience?

- Do they want to be there? Therefore are they receptive?
- Time of day – also affects receptivity
- Venue – affects receptivity
- Their level of knowledge and experience
- Attitudes and beliefs regarding you, your products, your company
- Size of group
- Time available and how long the key influencers can stay
- Who is attending and why?

58 Triangle of Factors

In order for a meeting or presentation to be successful there is a triangle of factors that need to be aligned. If one of these factors is non-negotiable, then the other two may need to change in order to make an objective successful. They are:

- Objective
- Audience
- Time.

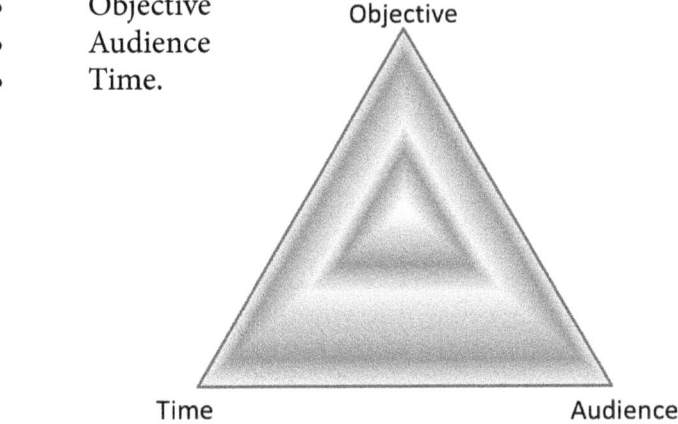

59 ABCD

You only have one opportunity to make a good first impression, so use the ABCD technique to get off to a winning start. Grab your audience's ATTENTION, explain to them the BENEFIT of listening to you, build CREDIBILITY quickly so they will trust what you say, and provide them with a clear DIRECTION for your presentation - people like to know where they are going.

60 Objective and Audience

What happens when you've planned a presentation to achieve a commitment from a group when the key decision maker pulls out of the meeting? If you plough on regardless then you're kidding yourself: you aren't going to achieve what you want. You should either change your objective or rearrange the meeting.

61 Time

You've prepared an hour's presentation and just as you're about to start someone apologises but tells you you've only got half an hour. Do you talk twice as fast, or have you realised the point I'm making? Again, consider changing your objective or rearrange the meeting. If you speed through it, the next time you're asked to present to the same people they'll only schedule you for half an hour and guess what they might say just before you start?

62 Content

What you say should be written not from your perspective but from the audience's point of view. Ask yourself, if you were to sit in the audience, what would you want and need to hear?

63 Audience's Perspective

This means approaching your preparation from a totally different angle than the usual "I've got a 20 minute meeting - what shall I talk to them about?" Force yourself to consider first what it is your audience needs to know and how they want to hear it, rather than starting from what you want to tell them.

64 Know Your Audience
What is their level of knowledge and experience? Make sure you pitch your presentation at the right level, using appropriate vocabulary.

65 Visuals
With the point above in mind we also need to ask what the members of the audience need to see that will help them get to where you as the presenter want them to be.

66 PowerPoint
We've all heard of and probably suffered from 'Death by PowerPoint'. It's easy to get into the habit of rolling out the same slides for every presentation just because we have them. Tailor your visual aids to your audience every time!

"My basic rule is to speak slowly and simply so that my audience has an opportunity to follow and think about what I am saying."

Margaret Chase Smith

67 Visibility
Your visuals needs to be seen by everyone, so before you speak check the sight lines from different angles. In other words, go and sit in different parts of the room and imagine someone listening to you. Can they see you, your screen, any flipcharts?

68 Beware Copy and Paste

Copying and pasting is a great technique to speed up your administrative work. How often though have you then failed to proofread the material properly and too late you notice that you've left another company's name in a slide? Worst still, have any of your clients noticed before you have? Tailor each presentation carefully to each individual company.

69 Interact 'Naturally' With Your Slides

Easier said than done! With practice the two techniques below will help you. You'll be amazed how focused your audience will be when you are using these techniques.

70 AIDS

A mnemonic that will prompt you to do and say the right things at the right time. Before showing a visual ALERT the audience to what you are going to do, INSTRUCT them as to what you want them to do with it, DISPLAY the visual and then SHUT UP! Allow the audience to follow your instructions and watch to see when they've finished.

71 TTT

Always TALK facing the audience avoiding the temptation to move to your flipchart or visual. When you've finished talking, TURN to the visual keeping quiet. Then TOUCH the visual to focus the audience on the point you're making.

72 Use Headlines, not Titles

Titles are boring and rarely add anything to your presentation. Headlines grab people's attention, they challenge people's thinking, draw your audience in. Think about writing headlines for your slides, like a journalist, ditch the titles, and notice what difference it makes.

73 Most Important Visual Aid

Don't forget you are the most important visual aid. How many times have you attended a conference, the lights go out, the PowerPoint slides come on and the presenter then reads everything that you can see! How much does that insult the audience's intelligence?

74 Words on a PowerPoint Slide

Many inexperienced presenters place far too many words on each slide, and when projected it is impossible to see the writing because it's so small. Think of the people sitting at the back of the room, and remember the old saying, 'Less is more'.

> "If you don't know where you are going, you will probably end up somewhere else."
>
> **Dr. Laurence J Peter**

75 Tip for Powerpoint (1)

You can create a laser pointer on the screen at any point during a slide show by holding down CTRL and pressing the left mouse button.

76 Tip for Powerpoint (2)

Use the 'B' key to blank out the slide when you've finished talking about it. Don't leave it on screen to distract your audience. When you want to display your slide again push the same 'B' key.

77 Tip for Powerpoint (3)

You can use the 'W' key to create a white screen. Be aware though that this can be a little too bright, particularly in a dark room. It's up to you what effect you want to create, though.

78 Returning to a Slide
If you want to return to a previous slide, simply press the number of the slide you want. It makes sense to have copies of your slides printed out (and numbered) so that you can easily identify the one you want.

79 Pointers on Screen
If you want a pointer on your screen simply touch your mouse (or equivalent) and this will bring your cursor up on screen. To disable the cursor use the right mouse click.

80 Your Ending
Have a blank or 'finish' slide at the end of your presentation. It doesn't look very professional if when you finish your desktop picture (along with all your documents and files) is displayed on screen.

81 Audience Interaction
Be clear with your audience at the beginning of your presentation about whether you prefer to take questions during or after the presentation.

82 Inviting Questions
If you choose to take questions at the end avoid a closed question such as "Any questions?" It's too easy for your audience to say "No". "What questions have you got?" is far more effective.

83 Question and Answers
Question and answer sessions will always prove useful to gain further rapport as well as gain feedback on how your message is being received.

> "Think like a wise man but communicate in the language of the people."
>
> **W. B. Yeats**

84 Time Limit for Questions
To help retain control, set out a time limit at the outset.

85 One Question at a Time
You can only answer one question effectively at a time so let your audience know this is how you want to run this area of your presentation. Don't allow them to hijack by asking more questions before you've had chance to finish answering.

86 Repeating the Question
It's often a good idea to repeat a question posed to ensure everyone hears it before you answer. You may want to rephrase to avoid repeating provocative or hostile words.

87 Use Questions to Achieve your Objective
Use your answer to the question to move the audience closer to achieving your objective.

88 Engaging Everyone when Answering
When answering someone's question ensure you make good eye contact initially with the questioner. Then move to the rest of your audience, ensuring they feel involved and engaged, finishing your answer by making eye contact with the person who asked the question.

89 Use Road signs as a Guide
Road signs can give you some great ideas for designs for your slides. Think about it - a road sign needs to be absolutely clear, obvious and instantly understandable. Are your PowerPoint slides?

90 Think like a Sniper
When it comes to bullet points on your slide think like a sniper, not like a machine-gunner! Audiences can't remember long lists easily so make your points concisely.

91 Avoid too much Detail
Detail in your presentation will confuse and bore your audience. It is far better to provide handouts later with the supporting detail than to swamp your audience as you speak.

92 Use Jokes with Care
The number of people who can actually tell jokes is about 10% of the number of people who think they can! Certainly use your sense of humour, but be careful about starting with a joke.

93 Preparation is Key
Rehearsal of your presentation will ensure you run to time (you don't want to run over your allotted time) and it will help reduce your nerves by up to 85%.

94 Mental Rehearsal
This technique has come from world-class athletes who will rehearse mentally before any event. It's been proven that the mind doesn't recognise the difference between a strongly visualised event and reality. When we think about an event we send micro-muscle movements around our body. If you think positively it will improve your performance and as a result your success when presenting.

95 See Yourself
The first part of mental rehearsal is to see yourself in your 'mind's eye' on the platform presenting. Make sure you see yourself looking relaxed, confident and powerful, and that your posture is really strong.

96 Imagine Stepping Into Your Body
While this sounds a little weird it does work so give it a go. Look through your own eyes on the platform. See the audience smiling, relaxed and reacting positively to what you are saying.

97 Now Feel It
Now add the kinesthetic element: sense how good it feels when the audience responds enthusiastically about your ideas.

98 Finishing
When winding up your presentation, you want to cue in your applause. The best way to do this is to change your tonality so that the audience has a definite cue to act on. For instance: 'That's about it from me, I hope you've enjoyed what I have said, thanks very much for your time and goodbye'.

99 Finishing Your Presentation
Finish what you say clearly, assertively, thanking the audience for their participation.

100 At the End
Repeat or state your objective, for example, 'And I hope that you now know...', or ask for their commitment or action if that's your purpose.

101 And Finally
Before you start work on your presentation ask yourself the obvious question: 'Do I need to do one?' Presentations are expensive in terms of time and unless they are done right are pointless and inefficient. If you attempt to do a presentation when you should be doing a report, document, or demonstration then you'll have an uphill battle and you will look like you don't know what you're doing!

So there you have it: 101 top hints and tips to make you the very best presenter there is! If you've enjoyed what I've shared with you and found it useful do let me know. My contact details are below. If you need more help in developing your presentation style I would be delighted to help you further. Again, contact me direct.

At the end of the day, presenting yourself isn't about knowing what to do; ultimately it's about being able to do it! This book would be a complete waste if you only learned the skills to make an effective presentation. The important part is to put what you have learned into practice. It's now time for action. Good Luck!

All of these techniques can be learned on one of my Presentation Skills workshops. If you would like to know more, please call me personally on 01789 400745 or email me at Steve.torjussen@btinternet.com. I would be delighted to talk with you about how we can arrange it.

Thank you.

Steve Torjussen
Sales Training Stuff Ltd

www.ingramcontent.com/pod-product-compliance
Ingram Content Group UK Ltd.
Pitfield, Milton Keynes, MK11 3LW, UK
UKHW021921060225
454771UK00026B/698